# The Tornado Is the World

## Catherine Pierce

Distributed by University Press of New England
Hanover and London

Saturnalia Books
105 Woodside Rd.
Ardmore, PA 19003
info@saturnaliabooks.com

ISBN: 978-0-9962206-6-8
Library of Congress Control Number: 2016944133

Book Design by Saturnalia Books
Printing by McNaughton & Gunn
Cover Art: Catherine Pierce and Saturnalia Books

Author Photo: Megan Bean / Mississippi State University

Distributed by:
University Press of New England
1 Court Street
Lebanon, NH 03766
800-421-1561

# Table of Contents

III.

*for Mike, for Sam, for Wyatt*

I.

# Disaster Work

Someone is on the plane
that noses 2,000 feet into the air, stops,
then drops. Someone is in
the tornado-flattened Texaco station.
Someone is on the bus the suicidal
or stroke-struck driver launches
through the guardrail and off the mountain.

It isn't you. You're watching
a ticker scroll placidly across
the bottom of the screen, thinking
*awful, awful,* and below those words,
deeper than articulation can go,
hums your golden gratitude
that once again this is a tragedy

you can witness but not touch.
You can continue the work
of chewing your waffle. You can
approach the smoothed edges
of disaster, and you can,
when you light on a rough spot—
the image of the little boy's

brown shoe in the rubble, the woman
who looks like your mother
howling in a blue hat—pull back.
Some will say this is cowardice,
your unwillingness to hold
these horrors in your hands. But
if you considered, truly, the dead child,

the husband that the woman
who looks like your mother
will never see again; if you considered,
truly, what it means that a plane
could drop without warning
with its full load of daughters
and coaches and magazine-readers,

that the sky might unfold a beast
that will hunt you without reason,
that the white-mustached man
behind the wheel of your bus
is not programmed but is a human
stranger you have chosen to trust
with your absurdly flimsy life—

how in the world could you do
the work of chewing your waffle?
How could you do the impossible work
of putting your child to bed,
saying goodnight, closing the door
on the darkness?

# On the Worst Days of the Fever

It occurred to me that I had swallowed
some shards of mirror without realizing it.
There was an ice fog that descended
and left me shaking. I began to realize that
I'd never actually held an entire conversation.
It was impossible. I had misremembered.
Bed held no solace. The night stretched
for acres and acres, but each hour was
its own thorny wood. I saw every number
on the clock. I sweated through one shirt, then
another. The bedroom asked, *Why are you here?*
*I thought you loved me*, I said. *I loved the other girl*,
it replied. I turned on the TV at 3 a.m.,
watched a special on *Hamlet*. Yorick's skull
was human, bequeathed by a dead composer.
*It made it so much more real*, one actor said.
My throat shrieked like a teakettle. Then
gray morning came. The bed didn't want me
but neither did the day. I wanted
to drink water without swallowing needles.
I wanted to stand without swaying.
The dried apricots glowed from the pantry.
Everything I'd never have again. Everything
that would sting forever. The sharp white
cheddar, the grapefruit juice. Galaxies beyond
my reach, the world was lit and spinning
like a carnival ride. Cars sped to Mexico.
Fireworks arced and shimmered.
Millions of people went surfing, dodged
bullets, sang arias, slept together. I watched it

through my kitchen window as my tea
rattled on the stove. Impossible that I'd been
part of it once. A squirrel plummeted
from a tree, shook its head, raced back up.
And I saw, suddenly, that the whole damn thing
was too beautiful for any of us after all,
that it couldn't possibly exist, and you'd think
I'd find peace in knowing I wasn't missing
anything real, but I only wanted it more.
In my fever I flung open the door.
In my fever I stood in the yard and reached,
tried to gather to my burning chest
the whole absurd illusion, the light and motes,
the fake bird cries, the lab-made pine air,
tried to hold tight against me everything
that had never been there at all.

# In Which I Am Famous

This endless room is deep blue, dark red.
I'm wearing my Valentino gown, vintage silhouette
but hand-stitched for me. It's the same purple
as my favorite twilight, just as I requested.

Everyone is here—I can see across the way
the black-rooted starlets and reality queens
drinking açai cosmos. And I can see the disgraced
congressman studying his notes at the bar,

his tan tie loosened. Slow-dancing in the corner,
the large-haired, button-eyed parents of the dead
pageant girl. I ignore them all. I am leaning elegantly
against a banister. My drink is a gin martini (up, very dry,

with a twist). My lipstick is sunset-cruise red.
All night, handsome, craggy men have murmured
things like *Hello, cupcake* and *You will be responsible
for the resurgence of the marquee* and *Your nose*

*is so legitimate*, and I've blushed in my practiced
unpracticed way. My three gold bangles clink lightly
as I tell about Monte Carlo last May (the passport
mix-up, the boa constrictor). Everyone laughs,

and their teeth gleam like china. At dawn, I know,
we'll head to Zuma Beach. One of the starlets,
hoop-eyed on Percocet and vodka, will drown
in her faux-fur boots, and we'll all be questioned

at the station. The congressman will slip away.
The pageant-girl's parents will weep large,
professional tears. Later, there will be a movie
about the incident. I will be played by a no-name

Australian actress with an exquisite doll-like nose.
It will be her big break. Soon, when she enters
the room, the dance floor crowd will part and she
will be the mirror ball, shining on us all.

# Imaginary Vacation Scenario #1

Right now a part of you is vacationing in a small gray
salt- and wind-beaten cottage on the New England coast.
In it, you spend afternoons shucking the clams
that here you don't eat. There, you eat
the clams. There, when the waves crash against
the black-rocked shore, you don't feel shipwrecked.

There is a sheepdog who sleeps all day by the fire.
You are companionable and he respects your desire
for solitude. The hallways of the cottage are made of books.
You're never lonely, and when a desire for something
human wells inside you, you touch an embossed spine
and are content again. In the cottage, you don't

remember skinny-dipping in a dark lake one August;
certainly you don't miss it. You don't remember
rolling down your windows to speed past a cornfield, the air
sharp with autumn's dying. You never even had a car,
and certainly you never kicked its fender in rage,
or loved anyone who rode shotgun. In the cottage,

the dampness never drives you south toward gold heat.
You want nothing, and have it. In the cottage you are
utterly assured. You know what the end will be.
The winds will blow, the salt will bite, the waves will rise
around you. You will stay inside the cottage and,
having given up on happiness, will be happy.

# What the Hour Before the Tornado Feels Like

Like damp towel left in the dryer.
Like crook of your knee plus school bus seat
plus busted air conditioner.
Like late August and dead horseshoe crabs
broiling along the shore.

Step outside and the air is a weight you bear.
Step outside and hackles rise.
Step outside and become dog: howling
is the correct response.

The sky is a bright eye
on an evil mannequin.

Silence, because what birds could sing
in those leaves flashing
their milky underbellies?

The wind is sweet but serrated,
like cider slipping over to vinegar.

Our bones weren't built
to carry this quiet charge.

# Heroines

The world was rich and wild
because we invented it.
Days were movies with ourselves
as tragic heroines. This copse of elms
the place the body was found.
This bridge by the schoolyard
the one spanning the Tallahatchie,
the one Billy Joe threw our baby from
as we watched, angry and complicit.
We twisted our hair and rubbed it
to breaking for the tangles we thought
were beautiful. What we knew about
lust was that it could make us shine
and that it would leave us empty.
We thought about what we would say
when the strange man approached.
We thought about what we would do
when the sirens swelled. We had plans
for escape, for Oaxaca, for Iceland.
We were, in fact, already gone.
We were riding a boxcar west.
We were changing our names.
We were scrubbing our blood-stained
hands in the creek while our mothers
called from countries away.

# Beach Town

You've come for absolution, but
the beach town has more pressing matters
to attend to. The beach town is busy
playing Journey from pink-lit cantinas,
busy scattering stars haphazard. You've come
for answers, but the beach town is absorbed
in perfecting the racket of Skee-Ball,
that old wooden clack-and-slam, and can't
be distracted. It's brutal, the way the beach town
won't cooperate: everything here is ripe
for construing—your parents did ride these same
carousel horses, the dragon kite is dipping
in a most interpretable way—but then
the beach town interrupts the shoreline
with a dump truck and a dead flounder
and what do you do with that? Haven't you
earned a sunset that reads as redemption?
Haven't you earned driftwood curved
like a *Y* for *yes*? You want the wind to be
a firm hand on your shoulder. You want
the biplanes dragging ads for all-you-can-eat crabs
to mean your life will be a bounty of plenty,
the found pink scallop shell your trophy
for Wisest Choices. But the beach town,
sorry, is not in the business of metaphor.
The biplane is a biplane. The shell is a shell.
You stand on the sand in early evening,
the sky shading to violet, the gulls screeching
over their pilfered French fries. At your feet
is a translucent whelk egg case, a cigarette butt.

The metal detector man wands the shoreline.
Behind you, midway bells ring and ring
as the calliope's song arcs into the humidity.
*Come on*, you say, *just give me something.*

# I Used to Be Able to Listen to Sad Songs

but that was before they started strutting
around with rocks in their fists, started
kicking the backs of my knees so that I
crumpled right there on the asphalt,
their faces streaming tears all the while.
That was before they started showing me
the switchblades in their boots. Before
the twisted arms and sucker punches.

Once, the songs slept soft beside me.
Their eyes were like moons
and they never closed them, so all night
I dreamed under lunar beams and woke
each morning sky-lit. But then I learned
that the earth is infinitesimally slowing
its spin. Then I learned that we're born
with more bones than we die with. The songs
started growling sometimes when I wanted
to cuddle. The songs started cracking their knuckles.
One morning I caught one filing its teeth.
That was when the problems started.

Now I armor myself in hand claps and tambourines.
I've honed a trigger instinct with the radio.
But sometimes I'm walking down a boardwalk
in the safe, bright sun, seagulls dipping overhead,
cotton candy spilling from every hand,
and there they are, locking step beside me
past the ring toss, the arcade. It doesn't matter
how fast I turn away. *Hello again*, they whisper.
*You can't run forever.* And then I know the ocean
is there but damned if I can find its crashing.

# Lesson

The lemon-and-new-shoe odor of the clean linoleum.
Your footsteps echoing against the walls
that weren't your home. How you dreaded recess,
where children shrieked and skinned their knees raw.
The treachery of the milk carton, its mouth that refused
to pucker. The day you made a birthday crown
for your teacher, asked her age for the gold numbers,
and she snapped, "A lady never tells."
Another lesson, like alphabetical order. That year
you adopted a red maple, trunk no wider than you,
and learned *deciduous, photosynthesis*. Your front teeth
knocked out in a wall-ball collision. Your mother taught you
pig Latin on the way to the dentist, your new blue dress
blood-soaked. Near Christmas, your teacher made you
try red Jell-O and you threw up. But you also
made a paper stocking—stitched with green yarn,
its symmetry perfect—and the warmth you felt for it
swelled you the entire bus ride home.

How did you do it? How did you learn in one year
that plants eat light and that the plural of *sheep*
is *sheep* and that when you cut a worm in half
you can watch its split body squirm away from itself,
how did you hold all of that while also the sky was starting
to take on a personality—benevolent on blue days,
aloof on gray—and you were finding that certain
Elvis songs made your insides pull taut in a way
that felt like an hour before dinner, and you found
a naked red bird on the sidewalk and tucked it in a shoebox
for your kind neighbor to nurse back to health but
it died anyway, two days later—how did you do it?

And now, here, decades into the fast future, here
with your knowledge of statistics and research
and Experts in the Field—do you feel any calmer, any less
like the sky could unfold at any moment and reveal more
hitherto unconsidered possibilities? Even now
can you believe zeppelins, anglerfish, all the people
you love who are every day out in the fracturing?
When you hear "It's Now or Never" on the radio,
don't you still sometimes pull over and sit there
on a side street of some neighborhood, clutching
the steering wheel and wondering when everything
will finally, finally settle into that storied equanimity
you've never been able to enter? You know it exists.
You've glimpsed it, in the cracked leather spines
of old books, in the sunlight that ripples on the pool's
turquoise surface, but vanishes the instant you dive in.

# Imaginary Vacation Scenario #2

You are, in this version, the kind of person
who enjoys being sweaty. You're never happier
than when your shoulders are freighted
with the 30-pound weight of all you need
in this life. You are backpacking around
a spired and bleak-skied European city.
On each corner, pigeons and statuary.
Each stone mouth reminds you of the lover
you left across an ocean and a dozen rivers,
the lover who might be, probably is, thinking
of you as you order the pain au chocolat
with a perfect accent, as you tilt your face
toward the rain in a way that says *I am the one
you picture when you hear certain folk songs.*
The men you pass on these rain-glazed streets
look at you but don't call out; the women
smile as if you speak the same language. The air
smells like diesel and the future: somewhere
in the fog there might be a scuba dive,
a daughter. You might try fois gras
or rabbit sirloin. You might take up
storm chasing. Your boots are perfectly
broken in. You read maps with ease,
are welcomed in lamp-lit taverns.
Somehow you always have enough
for cheap wine and somehow it tastes
like gold. In this version, your face is unlined.
In this version, everything is yet to happen.

## "Rare Winter Tornadoes Sweep Through South"

Here it is, not even February, and the boy
is going sockless, the birds are calling

with June-hot abandon, the sun is sincere
against the blue blue sky. Most days I forget

my coat and don't go back, while up north
the clouds are the color of the interstate.

In my hometown, heads are bent against gales,
cars are coughing into frosted mornings.

Down here we're crocus-blessed.
So I know not to complain. But I feel

each sprig of green like a needle. This
singing winter is an unhinged sweetheart—

all gloss and lilt, until the shift. Then
the temperature drops like a downed limb,

and there's vengeance, sucking up livestock
and pines into a sky suddenly gone

smoke-gray and whirling. I won't be sugar-
talked by the warmth. My red sundress

sparks in the closet like a warning flare.
Each day I wait for the blue to vanish

into a vacuum where no birds bother.

# The Unabashed Tourist Brings Her Lover to the French Quarter

Baby, darlin', *cher*—we can talk like that
here—let me show you around. In this place
you can buy me a hurricane, and we can
stroll all night with storms in our hands.
Let's pretend it's the Jazz Age. Let's pretend
there's no such thing as Pennsylvania.
Baby, just pretend for once! Lure me
with oysters. That sign gleaming gold—
*DESIRE*—is a lodestar. The streetcar's
a bus line now, but we can rename any route.
In this place you can rename me. Get me
an absinthe, I'm wearing my tall black boots.
I never wince on the sip, do I, because liquor to me
is smooth and sweet and I never stagger, do I?
No. That's the word you're looking for,
although here the word is usually *yes*. Say it
with me. Say yes, the abandoned construction
site at midnight. Say yes, your hands inside
my dress outside the blue-lit closed-up gallery.
Yes, the oysters that won't make us sick,
yes, the French words like sugar, yes, sugar,
in our throats, the riverboats with their cargoes
of diamonds (yes, diamonds—honey, my head
is a guidebook), yes, our eyes are full
of glitter and guile, our mouths spin
voodoo, I am gorgeous with my cigarette,
you're a gangster with your Sazerac,
the tuba player plays, yes, yes, just for us.

# The Unabashed Tourist Talks With a Skee-Ball Proprietor in Ocean City, MD

I'll tell you a secret:
I'm highly skilled at scoring hundreds.
I bank it. Watch. See?
I'll take the pink shark, please.
I'll tell you another: I want
to love the ocean, but it panics me.
It's not the water, it's the opacity,
how you could step on claws
or scales, how you could open
your mouth and a fish—or worse—
could drift in. Here's another:
I want to love that Ferris wheel—
its reds and blues are the colors
of my invented childhood—but
the kids kicking to rock the cars,
the suspension at the top while
riders unload—I can't take that
kind of uncertainty. Yes,
another pink shark. Here's one more:
later today I'll sit on a bench
eating French fries with vinegar,
though I hate vinegar, gazing
at the sea in the hopes that I'll look
straight out of someone's dreams
of what has been missing
from America these last decades.
I told you I was good, didn't I?
Yes, I'd like to trade up.

# The Unabashed Tourist Meets a Man at a Bar Outside Reno

You like my boots, don't you? I like yours.
I don't have a dog yet, but his name is Horatio Alger.
I'm looking for a ghost town with swinging doors.
Whiskey, thank you. I'm not particular.
Your sky is so blue it glares.
The dog I don't have is missing one foot but scales Mount Rose like a goat.
That pine-and-sage smell makes me an entire inch taller.
I belong above the tree line. Like a pika. Oh, I've done research.
It feels like the sky is closing its jaws around me.
In a good way.
If the coyotes lure my dog away, I'll hunt them down myself.
I'm practicing by shooting at rusted cars.
I spent today climbing. Tomorrow, too.
Yes, I'll have another.
Why would I slow down?

# The Unabashed Tourist Chats With Diner Patrons in Tennessee While Waiting Out a Tornado Warning

It's thrilling, isn't it, the siren's howl?
Nothing in my life has ever been urgent.
Sirens say the universe needs you enough
to holler a caution. So why the grim eyes?
Why the coffee-mug-clutching, the parking-lot-
watching? I know I shouldn't say it, but
I hope it comes close. I've never seen a tornado
and I want my own narrow escape.
You're from tough stock here—I've read biographies.
All those gunslingers and moonshiners.
They wouldn't watch from the windows.
They'd gallop at the horizon, hooting.
They'd tie the tornado down and make it beg.
In the movie I'm writing in my head,
I walk out into the rain and wait, and when
I spot the tornado churning across the fields,
I grin and spit and stay rooted.
That's the whole movie. But if I know
one thing, it's that the sky will stay empty.
Oh, why the moan, why the stink-eye?
I know I shouldn't say it out loud, but
aren't we all thinking it? We all know
nothing ever really comes close.

# II.

*EF-4 (wind speeds 166-200 mph):*
*Devastating damage. Well-constructed houses and whole frame houses*
*completely leveled; cars thrown and small missiles generated.*
                    —Enhanced Fujita Scale tornado rating

# The Tornado Is Sick of This Life as a Novelty,

a story for pretty girls
and bragging boys to tell
their fish-mouthed friends.
*We had just started dinner when*
*I had my hand up her shirt when*
*Our house survived, but all the eyeglasses / china / photo albums disappeared*
So many campfire tales:
chickens plucked naked,
goats in bedrooms,
trout silvering the cotton fields.
Always a cat who turns up
four days later three towns over, *alive!*,
always a woman cartoon-cowering
behind the front door of her gone house.

Then the stories stop. The world returns
to green and routine and next time
the sirens sound, that springtime drone,
some people don't even look up
from their lentil soup,
their Xbox, their laundry.

What can the tornado do? No one ever says
*Take me with you,*
except for one old woman and a teenage boy
but they were their own disasters
and the tornado has no use for sad sacks.

So the tornado will try again. The sky
darkens and brightens at once.
The tornado sees the father
buying cigarettes at the Stop N Go,
the dentist humming as she drills
a molar. Maybe this time they won't
tell the stories. Maybe this time
they'll tip their awestruck faces skyward,
cry out like children to be lifted
and spun.

# The Tornado Knows Itself

"Tornadoes have been colorfully described in many ways: a giant serpent with its head on the ground; the finger of God; a huge elephant's trunk searching for food; a monstrous snake, writhing, biting, and kissing the ground; a giant barrel hanging in the air; a great column surrounded by silvery ribbons…"

—meteorologist Thomas P. Grazulis

The tornado is moved by how
you try to explain it. So Biblical,
so romantic, the way you imagine it
appendage of your god, the way
you have it kiss and dance.
And the beasts! Fanged and stomp-
footed, rulers of their acreages—
the tornado appreciates the gesture.
The tornado knows, of course,
that it is made of wind and vapor,
but only as much as you are made
of water-logged cells. As you are made
of 1963 and one particular snow day
and your newborn's black-downed ears,
so the tornado is made of buzz saws
and black flies, of the word *riddance*,
of the moment the teenage boy exposed
himself to the art teacher and couldn't
explain why, could only cry in shame.
The tornado is made of everything
you can never love, everything you can
never look at without wincing, which is why,

in your naiveté, you write it,
sing it, talk it into anything else.
But sweet humans.
The tornado has no acreage.
The tornado has no hands, no god, no silvery ribbons.
Sweet humans. So hemmed in and soft.
The tornado could almost want
to keep you safe.

# The Tornado Collects the Animals

The tornado likes animals because
they pay attention. The tornado
sees the dogs howling up
from rippling yards, the cows huddled
mutely against one another,
a sparrow pulsing its wings hard
to stay stationary. The animals
stare and quake. The animals
slink low, or toss menacing growls
into the thick air. The tornado knows
the animals look up and think *o marvel,*
*o master, o strong one.*

Where are their people?
They have left their pets to fend the wind
alone. They are doing laundry,
buying liquor, sitting at desks, bowling.
A few are already bunkered
in bathtubs or basements,
as if safety is a human entitlement.

The tornado will gather
the animals tenderly, one by one—
the squirrel, the brown dog,
the shuddering armadillo.
The tornado will wrap them tight.
It will make sure the poor things
know what it is to be held.

# The Tornado Visits the Town

The tornado waits to become itself,
slowly turning above the interstate.
Radio words crackle through the air:
*major rotation, place of shelter,* but also
*that was AC/DC with* and
*so I said Lady, you can keep the ring!* and
*folks, a donation today will—*

This, the tornado sees, is a town
in need. Bankrupt of the fear
that makes life perfect and sharp
as a shattered plate.

So the tornado gathers itself.
Below, a few faces blanch in windows.
Some cars speed up. Some cars slow down.
The tornado dips and loudens,
rises, then dips again.
The tornado is gratified
to see a man cowering in a ditch,
a small girl racing from backyard to house.
Everyone is learning. The radios
are silenced. Then other noises
filter up into the turbulence.
A horse pawing at its stall floor.
A woman yelling *In here, Kayla, now!*
A litany of apologies: *God, I'm sorry*
*for last New Year's,*
*for refusing to visit my mother,*
*for calling the hunchback "the hunchback,"*

*for the accident, the spelling test, the six hundred dollars.*
A man whispering *Spare me, oh God, I'll make it right.*

But the tornado cannot stop. Will not.
The world cannot stop turning, and this minute
the tornado is the world. Cars lift like birds,
trees bullet, everything is collapse.
The tornado has no regrets.
Has no regrets.
Has no regrets.

# The Mother Warns the Tornado

*Scene: a bathtub, dry. The noise outside inaudible behind the baby's wails.*

I know I've already had more than I deserve.
These lungs that rise and fall without effort,
the husband who sets free house lizards,
this red-doored ranch, my mother on the phone,
the fact that I can eat anything—gouda, popcorn,
massaman curry—without worry. Sometimes
I feel like I've been overlooked. Checks
and balances, and I wait for the tally to be evened.
But I am a greedy son of a bitch, and there
I know we are kin. Tornado, this is my child.
Tornado, I won't say I built him, but I am
his shelter. For months I buoyed him
in the ocean, on the highway; on crowded streets
I learned to walk with my elbows out.
And now he is here, and he is new, and he
is a small moon, an open face, a heart.
Tornado, I want more. Nothing is enough.
Nothing ever is. I will heed the warning
protocol, I will cover him with my body, I will
wait with mattress and flashlight,
but know this: If you come down here—
if you splinter your way through our pines,
if you suck the roof off this red-doored ranch,
if you reach out a smoky arm for my child—
I will turn hacksaw. I will turn grenade.
I will invent for you a throat and choke you.
I will find your stupid wicked whirling
head and cut it off. Do not test me.
If you come down here, I will teach you about

greed and hunger. I will slice you into palm-
sized gusts. Then I will feed you to yourself.

# Holy Shit

This morning we took the long way
to the dentist, the coffee shop, the sawmill.
This morning we replaced the carburetor.
This morning we stormed out the front door
because our mother was nagging about our failure
to make a grandchild, to snag a prom date.
This morning we washed our baby's hair
in the yellow shampoo that smells like sunshine
pulled through water. We blasted *La Traviata*.
We deposited checks. We forgot to pack a lunch.
This morning the sky was thick but blue
and we said the same words we always say:
*Later, tonight, this afternoon, soon*. This morning
we took care as we handled the wrench,
as we braked just ahead of red, as we stepped
on the puddleless tiles. This morning
we knew caution could prevent disaster.
If we've known anything all along, it's that.

Now gravity has lost its bravado.
The sky is full of metal.
The lights don't work.
Now here we are in a service pit
of the lube station, in the freezer
of the Stop N Go. Here we are
in the bathtub where just last night
we soaked in lavender.
Here are the frozen egg sandwiches
and here the Pennzoil and here
the baby shampoo and here
is the gray darkness heavier

than any nighttime and we are
repeating the strangest prayer.
The words are anchoring us.
It isn't blasphemy.
Here is the roof groaning.
Here we are holding each other
down, knowing the sky now
in a new way with her mask
pulled off, knowing how
the air can roar and even still
wanting to stay here.
O, please. Hear our prayer.
We mean we know this place
is profane. We mean
we know it's sacred.

# The Dog Greets the Tornado

Hello one-not-like-me. Hello
to your great tail. You are larger
than the truck that takes me
to the woods and back. You are larger
than the house I sometimes go in.
I see you coming close. I am blown
back on myself. My teeth buzz.

Today I caught a squirrel. Today
I dug a patch of earth bare and slept
for a while. It was a good day.

You are so large. The man is inside
the house. I feel my haunches needling up.

And now the brown trees are below me.
The house is below me. The man
is below me. I am part of the sky.
I hear you howling. You must
have learned that from me.

# The Teenager Watches the Tornado in Her Rearview

Yesterday, tornado, I lied to my father,
a good man. I told him C. and I were going
to the game, but instead we were in a pickup,
teeth and skin, vinyl-sweating, murmuring words
I've been told are unholy, but god they felt holy.
We stayed till we turned to salt and ash,
and then drove home looking just the same.
Later, I found a seatbelt bruise on my hip,
and I stroked it as my blood pulsed
*next time, next time, next time.*

Now you fill the mirror completely.
All around me, the sky is somewhere
I've never been. On the radio, an ad
for Ted's Tires on 12, the woman's voice
light like she's never seen a wicked thing
in her life. The Tercel is rattling
like a tin can tied to a dog's tail.
I saw that in a movie once. Oh god.
I saw that in a movie. Once. Last night
when I got home my father said, *Goodnight,*
*my red-headed gal,* and I thought only,
blank with relief, *He doesn't know.*

# On the Origins of the Tornado

Once, a hundred Aprils ago, the tornado
was a young man being pulled along
by the Missouri River while his friends
laughed, then called, then screamed, then
went silent. Once, the tornado
was a fat tabby kicked by a fatter kid.
During the Depression, the tornado
rinsed and saved aluminum foil.
The tornado was once an old hotel slated
for demolition. Was once a penny
dropped off a skyscraper. Those days
were full of sweat and scramble. So with effort,
with fortitude, the tornado became
the Atlantic Ocean on a relatively calm day
in August, the circus tiger roaring
on command. For a few months, the engine
of a dependable locomotive. These were decent times,
but dull: always the same sound of the waves
and the tracks, the same applause and butcher-
carved lamb. No one likes being taken
for granted. So the tornado became
the heavy class ring on a bully's finger,
the eyetooth of the possibly-rabid dog.
The tornado was the Kool-Aid
to which the cyanide was added.
The tornado was a billy club in Selma.
The tornado was one pine root loosed
in the great mudslide. The tornado learned
that there was an electricity
in the percussion of splintering wood

and splitting bone. That fury
stills into awe, and what is love
but aweful? The tornado listened until
the howls crystallized into a ringing
song, a round. Ruin, awe, love,
it went, round and around and around.
The tornado listened, and then was home.

# The Mother Hears the Tornado Sirens Stop

*Scene: a bathtub, dry*

In the space left by the ceasing
of the sirens and her baby's howls,
she hears everything. The cottony sound
of her own breath ratcheting in and out.
The light fixture buzzing quietly.
The wrecked town outside
with its green mournful growl.
She stands, and hears her shins unpeel
from the porcelain: a comic noise
in some other movie. Her son's
small grunt of protest as she shifts
his sleeping weight. The next county over,
the rising discord of terror, clanking
like a thousand car parts. The small metallic
click of the brass knob as she moves
into the hallway. The hallway, still there,
droning its low dominant pitch
of shadows and neglected houseplants.
The moment before she opens
the front door: her son's heart
thudding against her own, its cadence
quick and even—steady enough,
she hopes, to anchor them both
in the new, world-strewn world.

# The Aftermath

A husband keeps opening his wife's purse
as if he might reassemble her
from Tic-Tacs, lip gloss,
crumpled receipts.
The checkout clerk keeps touching
her cat's small head as if to ensure
that the animal is still there.
When it sinks its teeth into her hand,
she doesn't pull away.
It seems feasible, suddenly,
that if one leapt from a rooftop,
the earth might relinquish its hold.
It seems feasible that
the two-year-old next door
might open her mouth and proclaim
herself Savior or Devil
and it would be truth. The grass
could be gold tomorrow,
the attics filled with bones,
the crepe myrtles along the highway
engulfed in flames. A stray dog
is happier, chasing rabbits
through a dirt field now clean
of the Dollar General. A father
turns on the radio. It's a song
from another life, so he turns it off
and—just as he'd hoped—the kitchen
is perfectly still again, as if no one
had ever dropped an entire Caesar salad
and laughed. A still-standing house

is blurred with green. Look closer:
a thousand pine needles
porcupine from the siding.

# The Checkout Clerk Considers Leaving

*Scene: her apartment*

Some states, she knows, are red in fall
and smell like wooded general stores.
Some states are gray all the time, so nothing

newly gray can interrupt their integrity.
Some states wave their flags of birds
and handshakes, some offer peaches on arrival,

some promise eleven feet of snow,
which is a danger you can avoid
by sitting still. Some states are up

where the action is, or at the country's edge
where piers are lit with Ferris wheels
and people still roller skate in short shorts.

Here, today, the sky is blue-dyed, but
the clerk saw the tornado, saw houses
splinter and lift away, as if all along

they had been made of nothing but twine
and toothpicks. Her car is in the driveway, intact.
Her suitcase, her skull, intact. The country

is open and roads are short. She could
be in Arizona by tomorrow. There,
she could watch the sky stay the sky

day after day after day. But some states
dry out your mouth before breakfast. Some states
are a tin drum ringing. Some states outlaw

certain dogs, some promise constant mist,
some grow ice as if it were a crop.
Across town, she knows, are live wires,

rubble, buried limbs. This
is a terrible place now. She watches
her cat continue the work of clawing

the red couch to shreds. The cat doesn't
mind that the couch is an ugly thing,
but then, the cat made it that way.

# The Aftermath (2)

How odd, the tornado thinks, that it isn't enough.
Even those massive oaks on their sides,
root structures exposed like an indecent lady's skirts,
even the slab foundations laid bare,
even the credit card statements still fluttering
to rest three counties over—you would think
this would satisfy. The tornado wonders
what it will take. The dentist is dead,
after all. An old man was crushed by his own bed.
Others, too: a teenager in her car.
A couple pinned by their loblolly pine.
Screaming ambulances carted the wrecked.
O havoc. O ruin. O what-is-deserved.

No one said *Take me with you.*
No one marveled.
Another failure.
Even amid the splintered wood and frayed cables,
everything is still green, is too green,
is not green enough. Someone has put his three dogs
out in the yard again. Someone has hung laundry.
And right now there's a woman
on her knees, giving thanks to God
and the tornado for sparing her son.
That's a good sentence to be in,
but the tornado wants to come first.

# What the Tornado Hears All the Time

Small rabbits squealing.
TV snow. The hiss.
A dryer tumbling an old man's one dress shirt.
Knuckles cracking.
An empty stadium.
A blood-eyed mongrel's froth and howl.
A thousand trees cleaved suddenly in half.
A match being lit.
A silence with a small tick,
like a bite onto nothing,
or a record's skip.

# The Mother, Three Months Later

Her whole life, she has ridden fear
like an endlessly cresting wave,
each long drive, each low cough
a possible death-in-waiting. So now
she is simply more focused. She thinks
these days about how the body
is built: marrow, bone, sinew,
muscle, blood. About the dead pulled
from wreckage and how smooth
that phrase is, *the dead*, how it doesn't allow
for viscera. She sees heart attack
in a red Pontiac, cancer in a blossoming
mushroom. Her knees crack when
she squats to lift her child, and she thinks,
*I am made of brittle things*. It's been confirmed:
the world's aim is to break.

One day, watching the afternoon
glazing the windows gold,
her boy climbing her leg, her house still
and sturdy around her, she blinks
and is back to crouching over the boy
as he and the sirens wailed,
curving herself like a rock around him.
She would have had her skull split,
her spine crack, if it meant nothing
would fall on him. In that hour,
her body was only object, only shield.
Suddenly, unforgivably, she misses that moment
when she was all deed and no thought,
when fear eclipsed fear completely.

# The Town Dreams the Tornado Apologizes

And then we woke up. And our uncles
were still missing, our azaleas yanked

and gone, our dogs dashed against oaks.
But before we woke, we heard you say

in a voice that hummed without words
that you'd gone too far and would hold

that rushing hole at your center for the rest
of your life. Hearing that made us feel a little

like church. We are people who forgive, but
who can forgive something with no eyes,

no ribs, no head to bow in shame?
In the dream, though, we sat and spoke

somber. In the dream, we reached out
and took what must have been your hand,

vanishing and damp. You let us.
And when your whir-voice said, full

of torn-off roof shingles and children's
coin collections, that you were sorry,

we wanted, with all our blood and breath,
to believe you. So, for the span of a sleep, we did.

# Where the Tornado Will Go Next

This mountain is a good mountain.
The tornado will cross it.
This river is a good river.
The tornado will churn it.
This yellow plain is a good plain.
The tornado will raze it.
This day is a good day.
The tornado will black it.
This house is a good house.
The tornado will wear it.
This man is a good man.
The tornado will keep him.

III.

# Ocean Block

Screams carry lightly on the breeze
from the Sea Dragon, the Paratrooper,

the Tubs-O-Fun. People in bright shirts
shriek and cling. My son in his stroller

is singing the alphabet, pointing out
fire hydrants and number nines.

I am willing myself to stay here
under the hot blue sky of June

instead of wandering again
into the dark hedgerows of worry.

In the dune grass is a mostly-gone cup
of chocolate ice cream melted

to a soup. The ants have drowned
themselves in the sweetness,

because what else can they do?

# An Apologia for Taking Things for Granted

When the finite dimensions of being alive
light up suddenly as they do from time to time—
when the famous movie critic dies, when
the office across the hall is one day humming
with gossip and florescence, the next day dark—
I resolve again to see everything
in Technicolor, to hold each click of a switch,
each pollen-thick day in my hands and know
its true weight. And for an hour, an evening,
I do. The earth trills and glows. The buzz
of the neighbor's hedge clippers a rich contralto,
the red of the tomato on the counter shocking luck—
how is it that I get to see something that red,
and eat it, too? But soon the walls—speckled
with flung bananas from my son's breakfast,
scratched by the gone dog I loved—begin
to swell with their own miracles and my heart
begins its galloping, terrified and nearly detonating
with gratitude it can't contain. The afternoon
is suddenly too gold, too mote-misted
to comprehend. My husband's question of spinach
or broccoli with dinner is a yawning crevasse
into which I fall headlong—the possibility of choices,
the greens of the vegetables, the crunch, the wonder
of appetite. Yes, I forget my expiring license,
my clicking jaw, but I forget, too, the pleasure
of a meal that is only and entirely a meal.
The insects and lizards and navy blue sky and moon
like a caricature of itself gang up and close in
until everything is blurred and muted, the street

a rinsed canvas, only my blood thudding in my ears.
Of course I wish I could properly worship
the nectarine. Of course I wish I could
give central heating its due. But I've learned
my lesson. If I can keep on half-hearing
crickets, at least I can keep on hearing them.

# Imaginary Vacation Scenario #3

Here, your skin shadow-laced by palm leaves,
the Caribbean softly gossiping at your feet,
it has never occurred to you to fret

over SPF or UVB, parabens or phthalates.
You never consider the clogging qualities
of the butter on your lobster. When the sun

sinks into your body, you know with certainty
that the entire planet is still—no mothers weeping,
no caught dolphins keening, no houses vanishing

inside a storm-roar of chaos. Everything
is green and calm and good, because your body
says it is. By the bar that sells rum-and-creams,

there's a butterfly bush. Its winged denizens
look like small pieces of drifting sun.
That makes sense here: the laws of the universe

bend for maximum bliss, and so the air
will never fog, the highway will never
be a highway, the cosmos might drop down

to halo you with sun-moths even as you read
your *Glamour*, even as you consider borrowing
the snorkel equipment, buying another rum-and-cream.

Later, gliding just below the warm water's
glinting surface, you see a stingray loft off
the coral-strewn bottom. You see its poison tail,

but you know it won't come near you.
It leaves a rainbow of sand-float
in its wake. Here, the laws of the universe

bend away from reality and into perfect
sense: the stingray, being beautiful,
could never hurt anyone.

# I Will Outrun My Own Linearity,

that blockheaded field guide: $x$ leads to $y$ to $z$ and back
to $a$, where $x$ is organic strawberries and $y$ is eternal life
and $z$ is fearlessness and $a$ is where it all starts again,
threatless, infinite promise. Instead, $x$ to a blue jay to this
French bossa nova playing in the alleyway coffeeshop to yes-

this-is-enough. Instead, the ocean to an acquiescence into happiness.
Or no, that's too easy. The ocean is everyone's enabler. So
not the ocean, poor put-upon workhorse, and not the desert,
horizoned empty promise, epic shortcut. Instead, catacomb
I've never visited in city I can't pronounce to gray mouse

half eaten by blue jay—no, by terrier (see, it requires
constant vigilance, this freedom)—to hubcap spinning
like the future. Now "The Girl from Ipanema"
is playing. "The Girl from Ipanema" is always playing.
That's why this is all so hard. That's why it's so easy

to snooze into expectation. Little bossa nova bounce, little lilt
so slight you're impossible to ride, how about I ride you?
You be in charge. Take us to trash heap, to aviary,
to Turks and Caicos, to mother-carrying-her-small-child-
to-bed. I'll barely hold on. You won't even feel me.

# Horseshoe Crab

Dear ugly one, I remember you.
You, over and over, pocking the beach
like so many war helmets, the soldiers
long vanished. Your many legs
curled hard. Your spike tail that I
always imagined as a beak, as if
with it you might speak.
You had things to tell me.
You had seen the depths and the sun
and then you died. You
were dignified even in ignominy
(your legs scooped by red-bellied
children, your tail popped out
for swordplay). I'd heard you called
a *living fossil*. I'd heard your blood
was iceberg blue. None of this
could be true, but it was.

I was a child already tired
of facts. I wanted a space flight
that didn't explode. I wanted
a clarinet that played colors.
I knew you were dead,
and even so, I picked you up
every time, your tail sharp
against my palm, and swung you
into the surf. And then
I imagined you restored.
Your crisped legs waving.
Your dull brown carapace

burnishing to burgundy gloss.
Your impossible blue blood sweeping
through your impossible appendages
like I had felt my own sweep
through mine. Your beak-tail swiveling
of its own accord, pointing back
into the deep, into the mystery-
country, where lived luminescent squid
and fish with mouths larger
than my body. I willed you to swim
faster, to go go go, your beak-tail
pointing you away from all
the idiot children who knew nothing
of reverence, away from everything
I knew, absolutely, to be true.

# Alongside

Sometimes, when I wake
after a sheet-kinked night
of tornado dreams and the boy's
crib-cries and sleep hollers,

I spin out a thin gold thread
of memory and run down it,
reckless, into other days.
Once, in a red-rocked desert,

the sun burned away everything
but the cacti and small quail.
Once, in Missouri, cherry tomatoes
grew like tart miracles.

Once, below a tower in Siena,
all of Italy sang hot and green.
Once, a white horse named Arrow
threw me into soft dirt and taught

the lift and gloat of survival.
Once, I curled on a red couch
and watched the brown funnel
come for Dorothy; the dread

lived in my throat for days.
Once, I slept inside haunted hours,
menace of my own inventing,
my parents' worried voices

humming through the vents.
And then despite my running,
I'm back where I started:
funnel cloud, a child frightened

of nothing. No one can say
to any of us, *It isn't real.*
What's real is the landscape
of the mind: sunbaked or rising

with mist, a forest in which you'll
wander forever, or a forest
in which you'll make your home,
wooden cabin in dappled light,

where you'll make peace
with both the slim-necked deer
and the screech owl who comes
most nights, whose voice

shakes the pines and who
you can know as another animal,
something wild, if not to love,
then to live alongside.

# Alleys

Because the proper *where* for an alley is *down*.
Because down them we might disappear.

Because once you read a book in which
a man with a top hat and a maimed hand

wept—not cried, not sobbed—in an alley,
and you've been in love with that man

for 23 years now and have told no one.
Because you secretly believe that being

Jack-the-Rippered is a rock star way to go.
Because your father said not to. Because once

you saw a movie where lovers in black and white
tangled in an alley in Venice, only the stone

walls keeping them upright, penned into the landscape,
though when you went to Venice at 20, you found

catcalls and bronchitis. Because if ever the 21st
century was going to open one way and end

another, it would be down an alley: enter
from the blanched Midwest, overdue

library books, the mundanity of salons,
and exit into blue, smell of jonquils, an old lady

with a strange accent scolding you *Child! Child!*
Because you believe there are still mysteries

worth risking a throat for. Because sometimes
your world is dim and smog-covered, and you

weary of it, the lamps never bright enough,
the coffee weak, and so you force yourself

into the blackest alley in town, stride through it
with your whole store of false courage, and emerge

into the same world, lit now by undark, unbrick.

# Relevant Details

The bar was called The Den of Iniquity,
or maybe The Cadillac Lounge—whatever
it was, its sign was a neon martini glass,
or a leg ending in stiletto. Maybe a parrot. Anyway,
in that place I danced without anyone
touching me but seven men watched
from the bar with embered, truculent eyes.
Or I danced with my boyfriend's hands
hot around my ribs. Or I didn't have a boyfriend
and no one was looking and my dance moves
were nervous, sick-eel-ish, and eventually
I just sat down. What I remember for sure
is that was the night I drank well gin
and spun myself into a terrible headache.
That was the night I thought I was pregnant
and drank only club soda. That was
the night I made a tower from Rolling Rock
bottles sometime after midnight
and management spoke to me quietly
but only after snapping a Polaroid
for the bathroom Wall of Fame. In any case,
when I finally stumbled or strode
or snuck outside, the air was Austin-thick,
Reno-dry, Montpellier-sharp. I don't remember
if my breath clouded or vanished
or dropped beneath the humidity. I don't remember
if the music pulsing from inside
was the Velvet Underground or Otis Redding
or the local band of mustached banjo men.
You know this poem has a gimmick,

and you're right. But understand: if I wrote
*Cadillac Lounge, boyfriend, beer tower, soul*
it would be suddenly true, a memory lit
by lightning flash. Who needs that sort
of confinement? If the way forward
is an unbending line, let the way back
be quicksilver, beading and re-swirling. Forgive
the trick and let me keep this mix-and-match,
this willful confusion of bars, of beaches,
of iced overpasses and hands on my hands,
all the films with gunfights, all the films
with dogs, the Kandinsky, the Rembrandt,
the moment the moon's face snapped
into focus, the moment I learned
the word *truculent*, each moment the next
and the one before, and in this blur,
oh, how many lifetimes I can have.

# Imaginary Vacation Scenario #4

You have a headlamp and a knapsack
of buffalo jerky. You will hike up the dark
mountain into the darker pine, you will pitch
your tent below a sky as thick with stars
as the air is thin. You are the only human
for miles, and this knowledge just makes
your legs stronger, your lungs more capacious.
You know how to skin a rabbit. You know
how to scare off a bear. The sea-level land
you've left behind glows radioactive and wants to know
your mother's maiden name, your preferred
birth control method, your views on organic
milk and GMOs. Here, your brain space is filled
with field knowledge: how to calculate distance
between you and the coyote's mournful yip;
the proper way to eat the pith of fireweed.
You know snakes can still bite hours after
they've died. The animals call and call,
their voices echoing through the rattling aspen.
You don't answer because they're not
calling you. You keep climbing. With each step,
the mountain grows and for this you love it more.
You will never reach the top. There is no top,
it spills upward and out forever. You could
climb forever. You will climb forever.

# Get Out

The new thing is an inoculation against
the scourge of fear, that creeping illness
that keeps you cowed and dull.

The new thing pricks for a moment but
then from the small puncture rises
a large red sun that arcs slowly upward

until the whole sky is, momentarily, full.
You need to go to Bratislava. You need
to eat raw oysters. You need that bright

shock when your seatmate on the train
from Phoenix, a man with eyes
of milk and rancor, opens his bag

to reveal a sniveling possum. It's not
enough to relearn basic French
from a phone app. It's not enough

to become skilled at baking focaccia.
These victories have the heft of tissue,
the thrill of an uneventful dentist visit,

and in a month you'll forget the past
perfect of *être* yet again. Don't bleach
your hair. Don't train half-heartedly

for a 5K. You need to get out,
is what I'm saying. Leave behind
the aspen groves or soybean fields

or strip malls of your life. The diner grits
400 miles away are better than the diner grits
in your town. In the place you end up,

Ursa Major will actually look like a bear.
You'll learn the odd birds that squawk
in a wisp-aired mountain city. You'll see

bottles of sarsaparilla in a wood-paneled
general store and stand transfixed
for a moment, over not the soda but the fact

of a general store. You'll find a ghost town.
You'll find the World's Largest Pitch Fork.
And suddenly you'll remember what

it felt like to open your window in May
and hear crickets for the first time
all season. You'll remember

the shriek-and-soar of the dipping
pirate ship ride, and how you floated down
each time safe in your absolute faith

in giant gears and fulcrums. You'll hear
a steel drum band at some Ohio dive bar
and your chest will open into joy.

Joy—remember it? It's that feeling
you have when a red sun rises out of a place
you never thought could house a sun.

# True Story

In the tales I used to tell, I was high priestess
of peril, and my listeners, I knew, hallelujahed
my every survival. In one, the car slid
to a gasping collision and I emerged unscathed,
miracle of teenage almost-tragedy. In another,
the rapids forked into a waterfall
from which I barely escaped. There's the one
where I dash across a midnight highway,
desperate for the ocean, as any reckless heroine
must be. There's the one where a pickup tails me
through dark suburbs. I spun the stories golden.
I iced them, I spiked them. I wore them
like wings, like leather. I never lied,
exactly. But now, years later, I can say it:
the close calls weren't. The car crash
a rain-slicked bumping of bumpers,
the waterfall so far to the side I only heard it.
The highway was empty; the pickup drove off
and I went home to a soft bed,
a dead-bolted door.
                             Here is a true story:
once, in a Days Inn bathroom in Cullman, Alabama,
I covered my four-month-old son as my husband
covered me as the tornado went by. After, we drove
in silence past half-houses, upturned cars,
pine groves as stripped and broken as if
an atom bomb had dropped. We looked
at each other. We looked at our son.
We looked out the windows and said
nothing. The silence said *caution*. It said *hallelujah*.
It said *no told story is ever true enough*.

# The Hawk

My son in his stroller doesn't notice
the clamor, continues his brook of syllables.

But in the tree is something prehistoric.
Something vast. Wings spread wide

as our kitchen table, massive head lunging
toward a smaller movement. I know

it's a hawk, but in our suburban neighborhood
it might as well be a pterodactyl, a dragon.

I've been thinking lately and always
of the ways we might end—me, him, everyone

we say goodnight to. All the blood phantoms
and texting drivers, all the thick-headed

tornadoes dervishing across our county,
all the ailments alphabetized on my bookshelf.

I've bargained and offered compromises
through every silence I can remember

for as long as I can remember.
Until the bird shook the oak,

I was strolling through a hazed future,
not unhappy, not afraid, but elsewhere,

away from the potholed macadam
and dropped horse apples, away from

the lilt of syllables. At the ruckus, I stop
and watch. I say, *Look, look,* though my son

is too young still to tell wild from routine.
The hawk flies off, something gray

fighting in its beak. In the quiet it leaves
behind, a garage door closes, a lawnmower

revs. Yellow leaves crunch underfoot.
We keep strolling and the street is the same,

only now it's surrounded by the world.

Thank you to the editors of the publications where these poems first appeared (sometimes in different form or under different titles).

*Blackbird:* "The Checkout Clerk Considers Leaving," "The Teenager Watches the Tornado in Her Rearview," "The Tornado Visits the Town"
*The Cincinnati Review:* "The Tornado Is Sick of This Life as a Novelty"
*Colorado Review:* "On the Worst Days of the Fever"
*Connotation Press: An Online Artifact:* "An Apologia for Taking Things for Granted," "Imaginary Vacation Scenario #4"
*Copper Nickel:* "Alleys," "Disaster Work"
*Court Green:* "What the Tornado Hears All the Time"
*Crab Orchard Review:* "Beach Town"
*Crazyhorse:* "Rare Winter Tornadoes Sweep Through South"
*diode:* "Alongside," "Horseshoe Crab," "Imaginary Vacation Scenario #3," "I Used to Be Able to Listen to Sad Songs," "Lesson," "Ocean Block," "The Unabashed Tourist Chats With Diner Patrons in Tennessee While Waiting Out a Tornado Warning," "The Unabashed Tourist Meets a Man at a Bar Outside Reno"
*The Journal:* "The Aftermath (2)," "The Dog Greets the Tornado"
*Kenyon Review Online:* "The Mother Warns the Tornado," "On the Origins of the Tornado"
*Mantis:* "The Mother Hears the Tornado Sirens Stop," "Get Out"
*Memorious:* "The Town Dreams the Tornado Apologizes"
*the minnesota review:* "Imaginary Vacation Scenario #2," "True Story"
*The Normal School:* "The Tornado Knows Itself"
*Phoebe:* "The Aftermath," "Holy Shit," "The Mother, Three Months Later"
*Pleiades:* "Heroines," "Relevant Details"
*Ploughshares:* "In Which I Am Famous"
*The Rumpus:* "The Tornado Collects the Animals"

"Relevant Details" also appears in *The Best American Poetry 2015*, edited by Sherman Alexie and David Lehman.

"The Mother Warns the Tornado" was made into a short film by Isaac Ravishankara for Motionpoems Season 6.

Thank you to friends, readers, and light sources Maggie Smith, Emily Spivack, Brian Barker, Nicky Beer, Nathan Oates, Amy Wilkinson, Chris Coake, Stephanie Lauer, Richard Lyons, Becky Hagenston, and Michael Kardos.

I am tremendously grateful to all of my family for their steadfast support of my work. I thought a lot about mothers in writing this book, and I want especially to thank the mothers I am so lucky to have in my family, in particular Debbie Albence, Felice Kardos, Sarah Reeder, and Julie Kardos.

My thanks to everyone who shared their stories with me, including Simone Cottrell, Jessica Flowers, Margaret Pitts, and Hannah Rinehart. Thank you to Dr. Jamie Dyer from Mississippi State University's Department of Geosciences. Thank you, too, to my colleagues and students at Mississippi State.

Thank you to Isaac Ravishankara for his vision in creating the short film of "The Mother Warns the Tornado," and to Todd Boss and Saara Myrene Raappana at Motionpoems. Thank you to Sherman Alexie for selecting "Relevant Details" for *BAP*. My gratitude, as well, to Bob Hicok, Simone Muench, and Aimee Nezhukumatathil.

Serious thanks to Henry Israeli and Sarah Blake.

Thank you to Mississippi State University for a sabbatical that allowed me to complete this book, to Caroline and Tony Grant for a Sustainable Arts Foundation Award, and to the Dorothy Sargent Rosenberg Memorial Fund.

And finally—thank you, thank you, to Michael Kardos, a.k.a. Mike, for making this rich and funny and strange and sweet life with me, and to our boys, Sam and Wyatt, for making that life even richer and funnier and stranger and sweeter. For every morning I wake up to the three of you, I am grateful beyond measure.